THE OLD MAN IS DEAD

Goodbye and Good Riddance!

Andrew Wommack

All emphasis within Scripture quotations is the author's own.

Published in partnership between Andrew Wommack Ministries and Harrison House Publishers.

Woodland Park, CO 80863 – Shippensburg, PA 17257

ISBN 13 TP: 978-1-59548-641-7

For Worldwide Distribution, Printed in the USA

1 2 3 4 5 6 / 26 25 24 23

Contents

Introduction

Have you ever heard the sinful nature called the "old man?" And when you're born again, that "old man" dies? Unfortunately, many Christians don't have a revelation of that truth but instead believe that the "old man" is resurrected every morning. They'll say, "I'm just a sinner saved by grace." But you can't believe that and walk according to the new person God made you to be.

Getting a real revelation that you have been freed from an old fallen nature will have radical implications for your life, which I'll be explaining over the course of this booklet. It is the opposite of what many preach today as the Gospel. That might shock you, but I believe it's the truth. The sad fact is, most Christians think that salvation only includes the forgiveness of sins. They don't understand that their entire *nature* has been changed, from sinner to saint! When you understand that your nature is no longer driving you to sin, your life will never be the same.

This is one of the most foundational things the Lord has ever taught me, and I believe that as you read, it will make a huge shift in your paradigm. As a matter of fact, one person came to me after I taught on this and said, "That isn't a para-*dime* shift; it's a para-*quarter* shift!" In other words, this is huge! It will transform your life. I really believe that.

Totally Brand New

The Lord woke me up at four o'clock one morning and really got my attention with the truth that believers need to understand that the "old man"—the sinful nature—is dead. We might understand and accept this truth on a mental level, but in practice, too many of us live like we still have this old nature.

If you believe that the old man still has power over you as a born-again believer, it will be detrimental to everything Jesus came to produce in your life and just stunt your Christian growth. As you think in your heart, that's the way you're going to be (Prov. 23:7). The way you see things on the inside determines how you will live on the outside. If you see yourself as basically the same person you were before you were born again—still captive to many of the same bad patterns and behaviors—it will be a self-fulfilling prophecy. You've got to realize that at the core of your identity, *"old things are passed away; behold, all things are become new"* (2 Cor. 5:17b).

Now, I'm not saying that you can't sin as a Christian. You might sin, but that is not your nature. That is not how God sees you. You are totally brand new in your spirit! Now you relate to God spirit to Spirit (John 4:24), not according to your old man. In your spirit, you are identical to Jesus (1 John 4:17; 1 Cor. 6:17; and Gal. 4:6), and your spirit is sealed (Eph. 1:13). That means it is vacuum-packed; no sin can contaminate it. When you understand that, it gives you boldness to stand before God.

Dismantle an Old Covenant Mentality

Many Christians have not received the full benefit of their salvation. They're so aware of their sin that they constantly fear God's rejection. They might not go to hell now that they've been saved, but they don't have any confidence that the Lord will use them or answer their prayers. That is a totally wrong understanding of the true nature of God and the New Covenant.

This is what Paul was explaining in the book of Romans. It's his masterpiece on the grace of God. He was preaching against the mentality of the Old Testament Law, where people felt they needed to perform in order for God to accept them. They believe that God gave the Law to keep it. But just the opposite is true: God gave the Law to show us that we *couldn't* keep it! It was actually given to show us a standard that was so far beyond our ability to meet that we would despair of self-righteousness and try to live the Christian life in our own power and ability.

God wanted us to just throw ourselves on His mercy and quit trusting in our own goodness. Religion has perverted the Law and told us that we've got to have a certain standard of holiness for God to accept us. (Conveniently, that standard fluctuates and is never quite clear.) But if we fail to meet it, then we come under the wrath of God or, at the very least, He won't answer our prayers or fellowship with us. Most of Christianity in Paul's day, as well as in ours, is performance-oriented. So, in the first five chapters of his letter to the Romans, Paul dismantled that belief. That's awesome!

The True Gospel Raises Questions (and Eyebrows!)

By the time you get to Romans 6, no one should believe that because of their own goodness, God owes them something. In fact, Paul's explanation of the Gospel was so strong that it raised questions, as well as eyebrows.

What shall we say then? Shall we continue in sin, that grace may abound?

Romans 6:1

Now, of course, the answer to this is, *"God forbid"* (Rom. 6:2a). This phrase is about as strong as you can get without using some type of profanity. It is an absolute unqualified negative: "No, we cannot live in sin. Absolutely not!" Paul was not saying to live in sin. That's not what I'm saying either. But I want to point out that when Paul taught on grace, this question about sin came up repeatedly (Rom. 3:19–31, 6:1–2, and 6:14–15). Most Christians would say, "That's a logical question." But they'd only be saying that because they're so hung up on sin that they don't understand what Paul was really talking about. So, he answers the question that he knows most religious people are thinking.

God loves you because He is love (1 John 4:8), not because you are lovely. He loves you completely independent of your performance. That means He doesn't love you more if you don't sin, and He doesn't love you less if you do sin. That's the good news of the Gospel.

Reason #1 to Live Holy

Paul gives two reasons to live holy in Romans 6. Remember, this is all based upon what he wrote in the first five chapters. So, after saying *"God forbid"* that we should go out and live in sin, he explains his answer by asking, *"How shall we, that are dead to sin, live any longer therein?"* (Rom. 6:2b). The Greek word for *sin* in this verse is *hamartia*, and it was used forty-eight times in the book of Romans. And forty-seven of those times, it was used as a noun (not a verb). So, most of the time when Paul mentioned sin in this book, he's talking about the sin nature, or what is called the old man.

The New International Version translation calls this the old self. Our "old selves" were the driving force behind our acts of sin. Paul was saying that since our old selves that loved to sin are dead, it is not the nature of us Christians to commit acts of sin as it was before we were born again. That's the number one reason that we don't sin. We don't want to sin.

Paul is making the point that you—a born-again believer—are dead to your old sin nature. But most Christians have been taught their entire lives that they *do* have a sin nature, so they struggle with the implications of this. To them, what I'm saying sounds like heresy. Most people's objection to what I'm saying isn't biblical or theological; it's practical. They're saying, "Man, I don't think I'm dead to sin. I still lose my temper. I still use profanity sometimes. I still lust." But, you see, they're looking at sin as actions and not as a thing. I will be explaining in more detail what Paul meant, but right now, I want you to know that the first reason he gives for holiness is that you don't have a sin nature anymore. You are dead to sin. The part of you that compelled you to live in sin is gone.

When you really understand what Paul is saying here, you'll realize that the power of sin has been broken in your life. You won't be sinless, but you will sin less. No one will ever be perfect in their actions until they go to be with the Lord, but you won't repeatedly sin once you understand this truth. If you are truly born again, you are—right now—a totally new person in Christ. You are dead to sin. It's only when you *think* you aren't (Prov. 23:7) that you will fail. When you have sinful thoughts and feelings, you'll just give in and say, "Well, that's who I am." But I'm telling you, if you are born again, you are no longer an alcoholic, a drug addict, a sinner! Your entire nature has been changed. If you believe that, you will wind up living holier accidentally than you ever have on purpose. That's the truth! It would radically, radically change your life. When I get to Romans 6:16, I will explain the second reason Paul gave for living holy.

Baptized into Jesus' Death?

In Romans 6:3, Paul wrote, "*Know ye not, that so many of us as were baptized into Jesus Christ were baptized into his death?"* Did you know that this is not talking about water baptism? Most Christians have never considered that there is more than one kind of baptism, but this is what the Bible reveals in Hebrews 6:1–2a, which says, *"Therefore leaving the principles of the doctrine of Christ, let us go on unto perfection; not laying again the foundation of . . . the doctrine of baptisms."* I won't go into all the different baptisms, but the one Paul is talking about in Romans 6:3 is the one that takes place when a person repents of their sins and receives Jesus as their Savior. Immediately, they are baptized into the body of Christ (1 Cor. 12:13), into His death. Their old man is taken from them and dies with Christ. This is a literal event.

Because people can't see the change that took place on the inside of them when they were born again, they have a problem with what I'm saying. They've been taught to interpret Paul's words as symbolic. They believe that the things he's saying will happen when they go to heaven. But that's wrong thinking. In the moment you received Christ, your old man died with Christ. This is a reality in your spirit, and it's the reason Jesus said, *"Ye must be born again"* (John 3:7b). That literally means born from heaven.

One of the reasons this is hard for people to understand is because many of the words I'm using have been hijacked by religion. So, when I say we are dead to sin, people think I mean we have ceased to exist or something. Well, no, that's never what the Bible means. I was raised in a church that basically taught I had to die to my old man every day because it was resurrected every morning. If you would have asked me, "Are you born again? Do you have a new nature?" I would have said yes. I would have agreed with the terminology. But I also believed that the old nature was dominant. So, I would get up in the morning and sit in a chair that I imagined was an electric chair. In my mind, I would strap myself in and confess any sins I had committed. Then I would see myself dying to each one of them. Now, you might think I'm making this up, but this is what religion taught me, and identifying with sin like that will lead you away from the truth. The Bible teaches that you died to the old man one time. This is totally different than what religion has taught.

In the book of Genesis, the Lord told Adam, "*In the day that thou eatest [of the Tree of Knowledge of Good and Evil] thou shalt surely die*" (Gen. 2:17).

If you look up the definition of "*surely die*" in Hebrew, both words are defined "die."[1] It emphasized the word twice to make sure it was understood that this was an absolute. However, Adam didn't die physically the day he ate the fruit—he actually lived 930 years after eating it (Gen. 5:5); but he did die. How? He died spiritually. This spiritual death was immediate, although the physical death was progressive. It could also be explained that his spirit was separated from God. That's what *death* literally means. Adam's spirit was functional, but it was separated from God's Spirit. Adam's nature was now sinful and of the devil. It compelled him to live in sin. The same was true for you before you were born again because sin passed to everyone through Adam (Rom. 5:12). Through your physical birth, you received a sinful nature (Ps. 51:5) by which you were separated from God. But that old man died when you were baptized into Christ and born again. Now you are separated from sin just like Adam once was in the beginning. But the difference is that your new nature isn't dependent upon you to remain sinless before God; that was accomplished through Jesus.

THE TRUTH YOU KNOW

Romans 6:4–6 says,

Therefore we are buried with him by baptism into death: that like as Christ was raised up from the dead by the glory of the Father, even so we also should walk in newness of life. For if we have been planted together in the likeness of his death, we shall be also in the likeness *of* his *resurrection: Knowing this, that our old man is crucified with* him, *that the body of sin might be destroyed, that henceforth we should not serve sin.*

When you are born again, God automatically takes the sinful nature out of you. But notice that walking in newness of life is conditional. It's dependent upon you knowing some things. Why? Because it's only the truth you *know* that sets you free (John 8:32). What is it you have to know?

> *That our old man is crucified with* him, *that the body of sin might be destroyed, that henceforth we should not serve sin.*
>
> Romans 6:6

So, there are three things listed in this verse: 1) your old man is crucified/dead; 2) it left behind a body that had to be destroyed; 3) the end result is you will no longer serve sin.

So, what is this body of sin that needs to be destroyed? The old self left behind is what Romans 6:6 calls *"the body."* Just as a person's spirit and soul leave behind a physical body at death, so the old self left behind habits and strongholds in our thoughts and emotions. The reason we Christians tend to sin is because of unrenewed minds, not because of a sin nature.

God made the mental part of us similar to a computer. We can program our minds so that certain actions and attitudes become automatic. For instance, when we were children, it was a major effort to tie our shoelaces or button our shirts, but as adults, we can now perform those tasks without even thinking about what we're doing. It's just a part of us, but in actuality, it was an acquired trait.

Likewise, our old man ruled our thinking before we were born again. It taught us selfishness, hatred, and fear, as well as placed within us the desire for sin. The old self is now gone, but these negative parts of the old self's body remain.

And like a computer, your mental, emotional part is going to continue operating the way it was programmed until you reprogram it. You've got to get rid of the old programming that was left behind—wrong attitudes, stinkin' thinkin,' and anything that caused you to stumble into sin. That's the only reason you aren't walking in the likeness of Christ's resurrection. How do you do that? You have to renew your mind according to your new nature.

> *And be not conformed to this world: but be ye transformed by the renewing of your mind.*
>
> Romans 12:2a

When I first understood this verse, it caused hope and faith to grow on the inside of me. Before that time, I honestly thought, *Well, I'm just an old sinner saved by grace. I may be forgiven, but I am an old sinner. I'm a failure. I'm nothing. I'm a nobody. I cannot make things happen. It's my nature to fail.* Then I discovered the truths I'm sharing with you, and it just changed the whole way I saw myself. I now see myself as identical to Jesus, in the spirit. I've got His power (Eph. 1:19). I've got His mind (1 Cor. 2:16). I've been renewed in knowledge (Col. 3:10). I've got His anointing (2 Cor. 1:21). I understood that the only thing holding me back from manifesting everything I had was an unrenewed mind. So, the quicker I could renew my mind, the quicker I would begin to walk in this new nature. I'm telling you, it changed my life. It set me free! You need to see yourself that way too! As you renew your mind to what God's Word says, you'll realize that it's your nature to walk in love instead of in anger—that it's your nature to turn the other cheek (Matt. 5:39) instead of hitting the other person's cheek. You'll start living a victorious life.

Now, when it comes to being free and being freed, there is a difference. Romans 6:7 says, *"For he that is dead is freed from sin."* We have been freed, but not everybody is free because they don't identify with the born-again nature God has given them. When I first got started in ministry, I was going to city and county jails and ministering to people. I remember talking to a guy who was just sitting on a bunk behind bars and saying to him, "If somehow I had the ability to free you and I unlocked the door, you would be freed, but that doesn't mean you'd be free. You would have to believe that what I'm telling you is true. You would have to get up off that bunk. You would have to put your shoes on. You would have to believe that if you stepped out of that cell and one of the guards sees you, they aren't going to put you back in the cell, give you extra time, and punish you." So, to apply this example to the Christian life, you've got to know the truth that you've been freed. You'll never walk free as long as you believe you're a prisoner to sin.

Dead to Sin, Alive to God

It's easy for most Christians to accept that Jesus died once unto sin. But the implications of what this means is not really understood. Romans 6 explains what this means for us as believers:

> *Now if we be dead with Christ, we believe that we shall also live with him: Knowing that Christ being raised from the dead dieth no more; death hath no more dominion over him. For in that he died, he died unto sin once: but in that he liveth, he liveth unto God. Likewise reckon ye also yourselves to be dead indeed unto sin, but alive unto God through Jesus Christ our Lord. Let not sin therefore reign in your mortal body, that ye should obey it in the lusts thereof.*
>
> Romans 6:8–12

Because Jesus only died once unto sin and He now lives, you are to reckon (consider) yourself dead to sin but alive unto God. There is no such thing as keeping your old sinful nature alive. You don't have a born-again nature and a sinful nature in you at the same time. That's schizophrenic! Sad to say, many Christians believe they have both and act accordingly. On one hand, they believe they're born again. On the other, they'll say, "Well, I'm still a sinner." I was taught that when I was born again, there's a white dog and a black dog on the inside of me; and whichever one I fed the most would win. One of the problems with that illustration is that people tend to identify with the black dog. So, when they are tempted to sin, they just submit to it because they don't consider themselves dead to it. But you aren't schizophrenic, and you don't have dual natures. Just as Jesus died once unto sin, so did you. You just have to believe that it was done! If you understand that the old nature is gone and see who you are in Christ, it will motivate you in your actions to become like who you are in the spirit. As a result, you won't let sin reign in your mortal body or obey it in its lusts (Rom. 6:12). This is awesome!

Reason #2 to Live Holy

Paul gives the second reason to live a holy life in Romans 6:16, which says,

> *Know ye not, that to whom ye yield yourselves servants to obey, his servants ye are to whom ye obey; whether of sin unto death, or of obedience unto righteousness?*

In other words, if you live in sin, you yield yourself to Satan—the author of that sin. In John 10:10a, Jesus said, "*The thief cometh not, but for to steal, and to kill, and to destroy.*" All of Satan's plans for you are bad. If you yield to him through sin, he now has a legal right to come into your life. But God will still love you if you're living in sin. You can still go to heaven, but you'll probably get there quicker because Satan will put sickness, depression, fear, and poverty on you. Remember, "*sin unto death*" means anything that came as a result of the Fall. So, understanding this ought to deter you from sin. Live holy; otherwise, the devil's going to eat your lunch and pop the bag!

Of course, Satan can't destroy everybody. He's going about seeking whom he *may* devour (1 Pet. 5:8). Cooperating with him through sin gives him access to your life. So, you need to quit living in sin for two reasons: 1) it's not your nature; 2) it will give Satan an inroad into your life (Rom. 6). These are two great reasons Paul gave for why not to live a sinful life. That's different from much of what you'll hear in church, but it's the truth.

Slaves of Righteousness?

In the same way that you were once a servant to sin, if you are born again, you are now a servant of righteousness:

> *But God be thanked, that ye were the servants of sin, but ye have obeyed from the heart that*

form of doctrine which was delivered you. Being then made free from sin, ye became the servants of righteousness. I speak after the manner of men because of the infirmity of your flesh: for as ye have yielded your members servants to uncleanness and to iniquity unto iniquity; even so now yield your members servants to righteousness unto holiness. For when ye were the servants of sin, ye were free from righteousness.

Romans 6:17–20

The word *servants* in this passage comes from the Greek word *doulos*, and it means "slave."[2] Once you were a slave to sin. You couldn't consistently operate contrary to it because your sinful nature was dead to God. But now you've been set free from that. You are now enslaved to righteousness. Most people don't understand this concept. They think, *Oh, no, nobody's forcing me to do anything.* But when you are born again, God puts His nature on the inside of you, and you are now enslaved to that nature. If you renew your mind, your new nature will compel you to live holy—the same way that your old nature compelled you to live sinful.

However, you still have a choice. That's why Paul is saying you need to yield your members as servants to righteousness (Rom. 6:19). It's because, as I mentioned before, your body will operate under its original programming until you make a conscious effort to renew your mind according to your new identity.

Before you were born again, you were a servant of sin. That means you were free from righteousness (Rom. 6:20). Does that mean you couldn't do anything right? No. Even a lost person can do good things. But nothing you *do* can change your nature. You were by nature a child of wrath (Eph. 2:3). However, the opposite is also true: as a born-again believer, nothing you do wrong can revert your nature to that of a sinner.

Now you have your *"fruit unto holiness, and the end everlasting life"* (Rom. 6:22). There are many in the body of Christ who don't understand this. There are people who believe that every time you sin, you lose your salvation; and if you don't repent, you're backslidden. They say that if you were to die in a backslidden state, you would go directly to hell. So, in order to avoid all this, you would have to stay up to date with any unconfessed sin in your life. I tell you, that's bondage! That's not what the Word of God teaches at all.

If people really believed that someone would go to hell with any unconfessed sin in their life, then as soon as someone was saved, why not just kill them to prevent dying with any unconfessed sin? That'd be the only way anyone would ever get to heaven. But that puts the burden of salvation on you instead of Jesus. The truth is, you couldn't do enough good to change your nature before you were saved, and you can't do enough bad to change it afterward. It all comes down to the question: Are you born of God? If you are, then you have a new nature that cannot be changed because of your sin.

Bring Forth Fruit

In Romans 7, Paul shifts gears to talk about how we were married to the Old Testament Law. It's another illustration of the old man being dead and gone. Now, while most Christians might have been taught that they're not under the Law anymore, it's really important to understand what a difference this makes. Why does it even matter that we are not subject to the Law? Let's look at what Paul says:

> *Know ye not, brethren, (for I speak to them that know the law,) how that the law hath dominion over a man as long as he liveth? For the woman which hath an husband is bound by the law to* her *husband so long as he liveth; but if the husband be dead, she is loosed from the law of* her *husband. So then if, while* her *husband liveth, she be married to another man, she shall be called an adulteress: but if her husband be dead, she is free from that law; so that she is no adulteress, though she be married to another man.*
>
> Romans 7:1–3

This comparison of our relationship with the Law to marriage needs some explanation, especially in our day and age. The way people approach or enter into marriage today is so far from the way God intended it to be. They just divorce and remarry. But Paul is saying that under the Old Testament Law, if a woman had sexual relations with anybody except her lawfully wedded husband, she was in adultery. So, the woman was bound by the law to her husband as long as he was alive.

Likewise, when our old man died, we were married to another—Christ (Rom. 7:4). For us to have an old man and a new man on the inside of us at the same time would be adultery. That's a strong statement, but that's what Paul is saying. We can't be lawfully married to the old man and also to Christ!

The old man has to be dead for you to receive the new nature from Christ. You can't receive a new nature while the old nature is alive. It has to die with Christ, as I've explained. Then, once you're born again, you're given a brand-new nature that is intended to bring forth fruit. In the same way that your old sinful nature brought forth fruit unto death, your new nature will bring forth fruit unto righteousness. That's powerful!

Romans 7:5 specifically indicates that before you were born again, you were in the flesh.

The Greek word for *flesh* in that verse is *sarx*, and it's not talking about your skin or your physical body. As a matter of fact, this Greek word is also translated *carnal* in the New Testament, which means "of the five senses."[3] The flesh is your mental, emotional part of you, which I shared is *"the body of sin"* in Romans 6:6. It's the part of you that is not born again. So, when you were in the flesh, the Law worked in your members to produce death. That was the only thing it could produce.

> *But now we are delivered from the law, that being dead wherein we were held; that we should serve in newness of spirit, and not* in *the oldness of the letter.*
>
> Romans 7:6

So, this shows the Law only exercised control over your old man, which is now dead and gone. Only after being delivered from the old man are you free to be married to Christ. Being delivered means that something was done for you that you could not do for yourself. You were dominated by the Law.

Maybe you're saying, "I thought the Law was given for us to keep us from sin." Actually, the Law was given to do just the opposite. It was given to strengthen sin in you (1 Cor. 15:56). Now, that's a radical statement. This verse says that we *needed* to be delivered from the Law because it's what held us in sin. And now that you have been delivered from it, you should serve in the newness of the spirit.

Remember, our old man is dead, so now we can be married to Jesus. We can reflect His nature and let Him bring forth fruit in our lives. But it all starts with understanding that the old man is dead.

The Law Was Not the Problem

One of the things that happened after the Fall is that people began to compare themselves among themselves, which is not wise (2 Cor. 10:12). They thought, *Well, Cain killed Abel, and he got by with it. God didn't strike him dead.* So, Cain's great-great-great-grandson, Lamech, comes along and kills a man in self-defense. Afterward, he rationalized that his actions were more righteous than Cain's because there was no malice: *"If Cain shall be avenged sevenfold, truly Lamech seventy and sevenfold,"* (Gen. 4:24). You see, he compared himself to Cain and judged that he was better than Cain. But when the Law came, it made it clear what sin really was:

> *I had not known sin, but by the law: for I had not known lust, except the law had said, Thou shalt not covet.*
>
> Romans 7:7b

Paul wrote something similar in the latter part of Romans 3:20, which says, *"By the law* is *the knowledge of sin.*" The entrance of the Law left no room for confusion, self-righteousness, or the idea of degrees of sin. You are either totally righteous, or you are a sinner. If you miss by an inch, you miss by a mile.

I once spoke at a prisoner reform facility in Okeechobee, Florida. It was operated by a man named Mickey Evans, who took in men who had been in prison. It was really set up to be a rehabilitation program for them. This place was in the middle of a swamp, so it was nearly like a prison itself. You couldn't get out without encountering alligators and snakes. And there were some bad dudes in this place: murderers, rapists, and drug dealers.

So, there I was—Mr. Righteous—about to speak, realizing I've got to establish some credibility with these guys. Most of the time when you go into a prison, people will use their testimony to relate to the inmates. But I told them, "I've never said a cuss word in all of my life. I've never taken a drink of liquor. I've never smoked a cigarette." Most people would think that is the exact opposite way to approach prisoners. But then I went on to say that actions aren't what make you bad; it's the sin nature. I said, "I was headed to hell just like anybody else. Even if you could undo all of the things that you did and never do them again, it's not just about changing your actions; it's about changing your core. Because of that, your core isn't any worse than my core. You just manifested it differently than I did." After I finished speaking, those men were set free!

Mickey actually made listening to my teaching mandatory for anyone coming through the program because it put things into its proper perspective. So many people focus only on cleaning up their acts, which they can never really do without realizing that God doesn't grade on a curve. Who wants to be the *best* sinner who ever went to hell? You either keep the whole Law without offending *"in one point"* (James 2:10), or you need a Savior who kept it and can give you an entirely new nature. The problem with trying to keep the Law is that it actually prevents you from keeping it. The Law increases your propensity to sin.

Once you understand this, you will despair of trying to live holy through the Law, realizing that *"there is none righteous, no, not one"* (Rom. 3:10) and *"all have sinned, and come short of the glory of God"* (Rom. 3:23). Everyone deserves God's judgment, and only He can justify the ungodly (Rom. 4:5), not the works of the Law (Rom. 3:20).

Now, this raises a question: Is the Law sin? This is what Paul addressed in the first part of Romans 7:7, and it goes back to the comparison of sin in Romans 6:1 and 15. If you understand Paul properly, it's logical to ask whether the Law is sin or not. But the answer is a thousand times no. The Law *exposed* sin. Again, this is not talking about individual acts of sin a person does; it's talking about the sin nature—the old man. The Law exposed the sin nature as vile. You couldn't change it; you were just stuck with it. The state of man before Christ was tragic. There needed to be a death to be free from the old man. That was the only way. And now you can be free through the death of Christ!

How the Law Works

Under the Old Covenant, the Law worked in you *"all manner of concupiscence"* (Rom. 7:8), which means "uncontrolled, unrestrained lust." So, when the Law said, "Don't steal, don't lie, and don't covet," it brought out of you a desire to do the very things it told you not to do. Let me use an example to explain this further. A person not being aware of their sinful nature is like a bull thinking, *I shouldn't be as mean as I am. I shouldn't charge people when they walk across my pen. I need to change. From now on, I'll be a sheep.* So, he tries to adopt the behavior and mannerisms of a sheep. But, as you can imagine, it would take more than a change in mindset and actions to go from being a bull to a sheep.

In order to be a sheep, he needed to be born as a sheep. It's a deception to think otherwise. All the bull needs in order to shake him out of deception is to be confronted with the truth. One sure way to do it is to wave a red flag in front of him. And did you know that a red flag doesn't make a bull a bull, but it will just draw out its true nature? That bull will rise up in anger and charge, realizing that it never was a sheep. Likewise, man needed a wake-up call about his sinful dilemma.

Now, God created you to be free, but you couldn't walk in it until you saw that you needed to be free. Jesus tried explaining this to people when they said they had always been free. He replied, "*Verily, verily, I say unto you, Whosoever committeth sin is the servant of sin*" (John 8:34). You see, when the Law came, your old man just went berserk. It rebelled against any type of restriction placed upon it. The Law made it obvious that you were a sinner.

Here's another example: If you don't like chocolate and couldn't be tempted to eat it, that would change if I said, "I'll give you $1 million if you can avoid eating chocolate for one year." Somebody might say, "That's easy-peasy. I can do that because I don't like chocolate." But Jesus said that it's not only about the dos and don'ts. He said that if you're angry with your brother without cause, you are in danger of judgment (Matt. 5:22). He also said that if you lust after someone in your heart, you've committed adultery (Matt. 5:28).

So, if I added, "Not only can you not eat chocolate, but you can't even think about it. Your thought life will be monitored," that would be an impossible task. When you tell people, "Thou shalt not," there's just something that rises up inside of them that says, "Bless God, I shall!" Even if I dangled the reward in front of you as motivation, you couldn't help but at least think about rebelling.

Let me give a couple more examples from my personal life. When I was a kid, I remember a time I was out in the rain, and the creeks had swollen. There was this log lying across a creek, and I dared a guy to go across it. He knew it wouldn't be smart, so he said no. But I just turned around and said, "You can't do it." I began to insult him, and the moment I did that, even though he knew it wasn't going to end well, he tried to cross the creek. Well, he fell, and it didn't work out.

A similar thing happened to me when I was running a race one time. It was a 10K—6.2 miles—and as I was finishing it, I knew I had beaten my previous best time. I was only about a quarter of a mile from the finish line and was nearly depleted of any reserved energy. A guy started to pass me, and he could tell that I was trying to keep up with him, but I just couldn't do it. He started pulling away, and then he looked back over his shoulder and said sarcastically, "You could do better than that." When he insulted me, it was like I turned into a rocket. My adrenaline kicked in, and I started running faster than ever. I passed this guy like he was in reverse. I finished the last quarter of a mile at a sprint. I don't know where all that came from, but I know that something came alive on the inside of me when I was challenged like that.

God knew the Law would affect all of us in this way. So, God gave the Law to bring us out of the deception that we are better than other people and that He owes us something. The Law gave sin dominion over us (Rom. 6:14). The Law showed us that we didn't measure up. The purpose was for us to say, "O God, have mercy on me because there's evil in my heart!" And it worked.

Apart from Christ

Now, if the Law made your desire for sin increase, then it's only logical that apart from the Law, there was no desire for sin. (That's what the latter part of Romans 7:8 says: *"For without the law sin was dead."*) But then in verse 9, Paul explains:

> *For I was alive without the law once: but when the commandment came, sin revived, and I died.*
>
> Romans 7:9

So, when was Paul alive without the Law? In Romans 5, he explained that sin is not imputed where there is no Law (Rom. 5:13). In the verse before that, remember he said that sin entered the world and spread to all by Adam. All who were born after him would have a sin nature.

However, there was a time when we were children and didn't know the Law and therefore, that sin nature would not be held against us. If we were to die in infancy, we would have gone directly into the presence of the Lord in heaven. That doesn't mean we were born again; it just means the sin nature was not imputed unto us (Rom. 5:13). But when we came of age—which is different for every person—and the Law comes, sin will revive. This is when, all of a sudden, we realize that we aren't just breaking the commands or instructions of our parents; we're disobeying God.

I can remember exactly when this happened in my life. I had just turned eight years old, and the first time I realized I had sinned against God, I got born again within forty-eight hours! I repented and asked the Lord to forgive my sins. The sin nature had been inside of me the whole time, but it wasn't alive or held against me when there was no Law. The time that the Law first comes varies from person to person. No one knows exactly when. Some denominations claim to have the answer, but I don't know if you can put a timeframe on it.

There are people with mental problems who may not really be in control of themselves. They could be thirty years old and still not have the Law come to them. But for most people, there is a point in their lives when the Law comes—they know the good they should do (James 4:17)—then the sinful nature they were born with will revive, and they will begin to experience death (separation from God). As I mentioned, this includes sickness, fear, depression, poverty, etc. From that time on, if you die without repenting and receiving the gift of salvation through Jesus Christ, you will go to hell. This is a strong reality.

So, by appearance, it would seem that the Law is at least complicit in reviving the old man. Some people might glean this from what Paul wrote in Romans 7:10, and it's a logical conclusion.

> *And the commandment, which was ordained to life, I found to be unto death.*

But, no, the Law was the catalyst that the sinful nature used to separate you from God. Paul wrote,

For sin, taking occasion by the commandment, deceived me, and by it slew me. *Wherefore the law* is *holy, and the commandment holy, and just, and good. Was then that which is good made death unto me? God forbid. But sin, that it might appear sin, working death in me by that which is good; that sin by the commandment might become exceeding sinful.*

Romans 7:11–13

The Law is holy, just, and pure. It is perfect. *We* were imperfect. Again, because of our sin nature, not only could we not keep the Law, but when the commandment came, we became exceedingly sinful. The Lord knew that the Law would have this effect on us, but He gave it to us so that *we* would know our fallen state. God was basically saying, "I'll reveal to you that you aren't as holy as you think you are." The Law was given to strengthen sin (Rom. 5:20; 1 Cor. 15:56), but it also had to be given so we would come to the end of ourselves and receive salvation. It's only when we come to the end of ourselves that we find the beginning of God.

No Longer Compelled to Sin

The following passage is a little wordy in the *King James Version*, so there's been some confusion about what Paul really meant. But if you can understand it, it will change the way you see yourself after becoming the new man.

> *For we know that the law is spiritual: but I am carnal, sold under sin. For that which I do I allow not: for what I would, that do I not; but what I hate, that do I. If then I do that which I would not, I consent unto the law that* it is *good. Now then it is no more I that do it, but sin that dwelleth in me. For I know that in me (that is, in my flesh,) dwelleth no good thing: for to will is present with me; but* how *to perform that which is good I find not. For the good that I would I do not: but the evil which I would not, that I do. Now if I do that I would not, it is no more I that do it, but sin that dwelleth in me.*
>
> Romans 7:14–20

Some have read or heard this and said, "See, this shows that you've got that sinful nature!" But that would violate everything Paul said in almost two whole chapters! Others would say, "This is Paul sharing his experience as a Christian. Even the man who wrote half of the New Testament couldn't do the good he wanted to do. He's bound by sin like the rest of us." No! This isn't Paul saying that his sinful nature was still dominating him; he already proved that the old man is gone!

He just said that if you are going to try and live for God by the flesh, with your own ability and power, you can't do it. Why? Because your sinful nature has programmed how you think and act. Even though you can affect it to a degree—with behavior modification and other methods—you are never going to totally master the flesh. That's the reason you'll get a new glorified body in heaven. It will come with a new soulish—mental, emotional—part (Rom. 8:23; 1 Cor. 13:12; and 2 Cor. 5:2–4).

You are never going to attain perfection in this life. No good thing dwells in your flesh (Rom. 7:18), so it's always going to fall short to some degree. However, Jesus Christ is in your born-again spirit (Gal. 2:20), and He *is* a good thing. Some people want to quote Isaiah 64:6, which says that *"all our righteousnesses are as filthy rags,"* but Jesus is now your righteousness. First Corinthians 1:30 says that He *"is made unto [you] wisdom, and righteousness, and sanctification, and redemption."* Now, to say your born-again righteousness is as a filthy rag is to call Jesus a filthy rag. That isn't accurate. You've got to start from the place that in your spirit, you *are* righteous. As you let your spirit manifest through your soul and your body, you will see newness of life manifest through you, including love, joy, peace, healing, and prosperity.

So, in this passage of Romans 7, Paul was writing that if you could remove the spirit and look at things only from a physical, natural standpoint, you would find that you are just as incapable of living for God as you were before you were born again. The Christian life isn't just difficult; it's impossible! It's only through the Spirit of God that you can do all things (Phil. 4:13). As I've explained throughout this booklet, you have to renew your mind to who you are in the spirit.

As a born-again believer, you no longer have a nature to sin; however, there is a law that's working against your new nature. It's called the law of sin, and it always fights against you. It works against your mind. That's the battlefield. If it wins there, you will manifest the old nature. Paul wrote about it here:

> *I find then a law, that, when I would do good, evil is present with me. For I delight in the law of God after the inward man: But I see another law in my members, warring against the law of my mind, and bringing me into captivity to the law of sin which is in my members. O wretched man that I am! who shall deliver me from the body of this death?*
>
> Romans 7:21–24

Again, this is not the apostle Paul saying that after all his years as a Christian, he's just a wretched man. No, he was a powerful man of God in the spirit! But left to himself and apart from Christ, Paul was a wretched man. I can say the same thing about myself. God has done a lot of good things in me. I've seen some awesome things, but it's all because of Jesus. That's how Paul answers the dilemma of a man operating apart from Christ:

> *I thank God through Jesus Christ our Lord. So then with the mind I myself serve the law of God; but with the flesh the law of sin.* There is *therefore now no condemnation to them which are in Christ Jesus, who walk not after the flesh, but after the Spirit. For the law of the Spirit of life in Christ Jesus hath made me free from the law of sin and death.*
>
> Romans 7:25–8:2

This is powerful! The law of the Spirit of life has made you free from the law of sin and death! If you're born again, you are not compelled to sin anymore! If you're still struggling, it's because you haven't renewed your mind to the new you on the inside. Here's another way of looking at this: In

Romans 7, the word *spirit* is only used once, and it's talking about a mental disposition not your born-again spirit. But in Romans 8, *spirit* is used over twenty times, referring to either your spirit or God's Spirit, where Paul further explains the benefits of living by the Spirit. It's just awesome! Romans 7 is filled with struggle and confusion. Romans 8 is full of victory. That's the contrast between trying to serve God through our flesh and living a victorious life through our new, born-again spirit.

Conclusion

I encourage you to renew your mind to who you are in the spirit as quickly as you can. You're going to start experiencing this life and peace that Paul goes on to talk about in Romans 8:6:

> *For to be carnally minded is death; but to be spiritually minded* is *life and peace.*

It is a process, but it's well worth it. You'll see things begin to change around you: your health, your finances, your emotions, your marriage. It's the key to everything in the Christian life. This is what God has done in me, and it's changed my life forever. I know He will do the same in you.

FURTHER STUDY

If you enjoyed this booklet and would like to learn more about some of the things I've shared, I suggest my teachings:

- *The Old Man Is Dead* (complete teaching)
- *Romans: Paul's Masterpiece on Grace*
- *Spirit, Soul, and Body*
- *The New You & The Holy Spirit*

These teachings are available for free at **awmi.net**, or they can be purchased at **awmi.net/store**.

Receive Jesus as Your Savior

Choosing to receive Jesus Christ as your Lord and Savior is the most important decision you'll ever make!

God's Word promises, "*That if thou shalt confess with thy mouth the Lord Jesus, and shalt believe in thine heart that God hath raised him from the dead, thou shalt be saved. For with the heart man believeth unto righteousness; and with the mouth confession is made unto salvation*" (Rom. 10:9–10). "*For whosoever shall call upon the name of the Lord shall be saved*" (Rom. 10:13). By His grace, God has already done everything to provide salvation. Your part is simply to believe and receive.

Pray out loud: "Jesus, I acknowledge that I've sinned and need to receive what you did for the forgiveness of my sins. I confess that You are my Lord and Savior. I believe in my heart that God raised You from the dead. By faith in Your Word, I receive salvation now. Thank You for saving me."

The very moment you commit your life to Jesus Christ, the truth of His Word instantly comes to pass in your spirit. Now that you're born again, there's a brand-new you!

Please contact us and let us know that you've prayed to receive Jesus as your Savior. We'd like to send you some free materials to help you on your new journey. Call our Helpline: **719-635-1111** (available 24 hours a day, seven days a week) to speak to a staff member who is here to help you understand and grow in your new relationship with the Lord.

Welcome to your new life!

RECEIVE THE HOLY SPIRIT

As His child, your loving heavenly Father wants to give you the supernatural power you need to live a new life. "*For every one that asketh receiveth; and he that seeketh findeth; and to him that knocketh it shall be opened…how much more shall* your *heavenly Father give the Holy Spirit to them that ask him?*" (Luke 11:10–13).

All you have to do is ask, believe, and receive! Pray this: "Father, I recognize my need for Your power to live a new life. Please fill me with Your Holy Spirit. By faith, I receive it right now. Thank You for baptizing me. Holy Spirit, You are welcome in my life."

Some syllables from a language you don't recognize will rise up from your heart to your mouth (1 Cor. 14:14). As you speak them out loud by faith, you're releasing God's power from within and building yourself up in the spirit (1 Cor. 14:4). You can do this whenever and wherever you like.

It doesn't really matter whether you felt anything or not when you prayed to receive the Lord and His Spirit. If you believed in your heart that you received, then God's Word promises you did. "*Therefore I say unto you, What things soever ye desire, when ye pray, believe that ye receive* them, *and ye shall have* them" (Mark 11:24). God always honors His Word—believe it!

We would like to rejoice with you, pray with you, and answer any questions to help you understand more fully what has taken place in your life!

Please contact us to let us know that you've prayed to be filled with the Holy Spirit and to request the book *The New You & the Holy Spirit*. This book will explain in more detail about the benefits of being filled with the Holy Spirit and speaking in tongues. Call our Helpline: **719-635-1111** (available 24 hours a day, seven days a week).

Call for Prayer

If you need prayer for any reason, you can call our Helpline, 24 hours a day, seven days a week at **719-635-1111**. A trained prayer minister will answer your call and pray with you.

Every day, we receive testimonies of healings and other miracles from our Helpline, and we are ministering God's nearly-too-good-to-be-true message of the Gospel to more people than ever. So, I encourage you to call today!

About the Author

Andrew Wommack's life was forever changed the moment he encountered the supernatural love of God on March 23, 1968. As a renowned Bible teacher and author, Andrew has made it his mission to change the way the world sees God.

Andrew's vision is to go as far and deep with the Gospel as possible. His message goes far through the *Gospel Truth* television program, which is available to over half the world's population. The message goes deep through discipleship at Charis Bible College, headquartered in Woodland Park, Colorado. Founded in 1994, Charis has campuses across the United States and around the globe.

Andrew also has an extensive library of teaching materials in print, audio, and video. More than 200,000 hours of free teachings can be accessed at **awmi.net**.

Endnotes

1 *Strong's Definitions*, s.v. "מוּת," ("*mûṯ*"). Accessed July 31, 2023, https://www.blueletterbible.org/lexicon/h4191/kjv/wlc/0-1/.

2 *Strong's Definitions*, s.v. "δοῦλος," ("*doulos*"). Accessed July 31, 2023, https://www.blueletterbible.org/lexicon/g1401/kjv/tr/0-1/.

3 *Strong's Definitions*, s.v., "σάρξ," ("*sarx*"). Accessed August 1, 2023, https://www.blueletterbible.org/lexicon/g4561/kjv/tr/0-1/.

Contact Information

Andrew Wommack Ministries, Inc.

PO Box 3333
Colorado Springs, CO 80934-3333
info@awmi.net
awmi.net

Helpline: 719-635-1111 (available 24/7)

Charis Bible College

info@charisbiblecollege.org
844-360-9577
CharisBibleCollege.org

For a complete list of all of our offices,
visit **awmi.net/contact-us**.

Connect with us on social media.